THE RHYMING REMINDER

GREGORY HEARY

NO PAGE IN YOUR BOOK OF DEEDS ON THE DAY OF TERROR SHOULD BE BLANK OR WASTED WITH SINS EVEN IF IT IS ERASED BY ALLAH DUE TO REPENTANCE.

As the eyes are vulnerable to everything they read, for which lowering the gaze is a true life-saving human need, Allah warns us all to prevent bad deeds. The need to focus on hasanat and blessings in all big and minor things is the best practice for a slave sincerely striving to succeed. So, reading things that are haram, or of less hasanat, is a Satanic trap to slip us up damaging our soul that starts to rot.

We were advised and made a great mistake one day while in the masjid inshallah seeking Allah's face.

I had asked about book topics we should read. Since the akhirah is so important then isn't Islamic ilm all we need? I was told we would get bored and that we needed a healthy balance. Yet while correct in technicality the liberality of having lack of taqwa led me far astray.

I was told to start my studies internalizing the Quran, even if just in my mother's tongue non-Arab interpretation. This was great advice for me as Allah decreed that saved me from a lot. Yet not for very long for it was time for me to grow, and though I came to know some things it was not destiny yet to go. Though now I have remembered it, such past advice to diversify could set many back. It is something that was destined so no point despairing on our past.

Recently I learned the heart is often hurt and locked by us ourselves. Whenever we crazily choose to do what we know harms our soul. To tell you what I mean I must explain some "easy" sins. Such as hearing evil knowingly, or through the eyes for fun. Sometimes it's differently camouflaged like the famous "compromised haram". The type where haram comes up but it's not the center of attention. Such as learning global news, that is not a matter of your jurisdiction. Your peasant views don't matter, such ignorance protects your faith. For wasting time is sinful and there is nothing you can change, except the types of crimes you yourself will do today.

Not knowing things that don't concern you helps you gain power over things you can control, which really matter. While revealing your real role, in worshipping our Creator. Avoiding sinful news updates grants you spiritual understanding you can't get otherwise. For Allah has sent knowledge between the lines which many memorize. Of which fiqh is only given to those with sincere taqwa they try to hide. There is a certain wisdom Allah indeed provides that is not heretical or unlawful yet seems crazy to most eyes. That prize is only tasted the more you start to rise. Everyone is unequal, yet all of Allah's words apply reporting more ilm daily to those blessed by the Divine.

Iblis throws whispers of false understanding cloaked in Islamic clothes onto those literate yet unblessed, to limit the benefits of friendship with Allah to whoever tries to come close. How do we get more blessings and raise in rank higher in paradise? By maximizing obedience in what you know already in this trivial life, which your limbs often deny as you comply with what's inside. For true beliefs within are always mobilized. And any sin can set you back, even ignorant ones done by mistake. So never take evil lightly, for every darkness concerning your faith is great. When you sin and know its wrong its even harder to repent, or stand before Allah again without more shame and guilt. Repentance should be a last resort lifeboat, not the only good deed you do. How many sins do you think it costs to earn hellfire specifically for you? Do you expect special treatment? Have you a exclusive Covenant? Or are you arrogant despite your knowledge and want to test the limits of the King? Pure beneficial faith is like a spark growing into a flame. It hopes to grow further into fire purifying the soul, heart and brain. Then burn every evil thing within to perhaps prevent your sins. So perhaps if Allah shows you mercy your body and soul won't be burnt again. But do you listen or reflect upon any good message you're given?

When we in the grave there is nothing left to say, for speech then will only benefit those given Allah's mercy. One point I must over-stress, though in truth deen has no such official creed, is that fiqh of understanding can come to non-Arabs easily. Just knowing Arabic Tajweed with perfect scholastic fluency, and knowing all the tafsir as reported by the Salaf, is not true understanding; if Allah does not bless it. Such special blessings are given by Allah to you, only if you do what you are knowingly told to do. Such as establishing Salat, none of us has gotten right. But I must comment on your past, to help you see the light. For Allah remembers everything though you forget in time. Allah knows best, I don't abuse, I intend to teach the truth. For we can lose a spot in paradise due to one sin of our youth. One sin we don't remember can devastate our record. The crime you forgot to regret can prevent future blessings from worship. As punishment for that, you will fall off the path. And not all such losers go to hell forever as kuffar. But because of falling off the rope of Allah while climbing, they land damaged. They can't ever get back up, nor soar again as highly as before, even if they make sincere Taubah. This dunya is a

store so don't sell your soul so cheap
without fighting. For the taqwa that
leads to safety is not acquired by
brushing your teeth.   Just using a
siwak, to shiny up the mouth,
"following the sunnah" is not what
Islam is all about. To taste iman as
Allah demands of all his awliya,
requires obeying what you know of
from the tiny bit you learn. Levels of
all creatures differ and lower levels
feel like hell, for those who get above
their standard level but it is
impossible to tell. Just as Kuffar and
Muslims cannot explain their huge
gap. The many degrees in paradise
make lower levels seem like crap. All

will be happy if they arrive, but what you lost will not be known to you ever, even when you die. Allah will only bless your life, when you truly strive, and give you deeper insight than those who read and write. For the brightness of spiritual guidance is fragile despite its powerful might.

Good Advice only benefits those whom Allah strikes, with mercy and his favor, filling them with light. Though kafirs call Muslims slurs which are too sinful to repeat. When you fail to live accordingly to Islam, that is your true defeat. You think you are on high when you do not recognize, the truly Great and Powerful Master who created a perfect sky. You think you know the Ayat because it's memorized, but the deeds done by all of us do not match our lies. Surprises are for devils which is a label you deserve applied. Yet even if you admit you're bad you've been much worse than whatever you've said. For have you not forgotten forgetting all the crimes you did?

Had you known Aqeedah and practiced Salafiyyah, as so many Muslims claim, what sin would you commit on purpose? Is not sinning any sin insane?

The inner guilt of sins you earn by betraying what you learn, will set you upon a track of nifaq until you eternally burn. Not all Munafiqs know it, nor can it be proven well, even if all their records show. Many Muslims ignore this on TV, Internet or Phone, or in their homes even if not alone. All sins of evil count as big, as said above the Throne. When you do what you know is wrong blaming it on the era, this is you falsely covering up your truly wretched failure. You will answer to Allah who will inform you of your lies. Such lies will only grow in size until the ships capsize. Then drowning will occur and you will die and not realize. By getting wet on purpose, just because you have rainy days, it gives no license for your crime spree done in Allah's name.

Even the "good" you do is truly worth much shame. If you only knew as much as the One who made your toxic brain. Those souls Allah unlocks from their many self-made chains, will surely be called insane or strange. Not just by Kafirs and the sinners but also pious folk of fame. For truly no one qualifies to understand the name, of what Taqwa is or many things, for all of us play bad games. They cheat themselves all day, all life, all throughout the whole timeline. And they would say this voice is mad because of so much rhyme. The ones who truly know Allah slightly try to hide. Because they know that once they know, telling others is suicide. For how can Allah teach a fool to read between the lines, to get the fiqh of understanding, when they're living such big lies? You've read Quran so many times, reciting perfectly what you hear, yet not once even when you cried have you ever truly feared!

The blessings of Allah came to you and were not recognized, so you died inside. But why? Why? Is it just the timing that made you fail to strive? No. They should not be surprised for they know the book with pride. So why are they still sinning while knowing how to guide? Because of truth they fear to hide, while Allah's plans are wise. Just wait for your demise for then you get surprised!

For Allah is truly greater, so much better than non-gods know. The Quran has letters which are protected as is known to most. Yet the huffaz memorize verses too fast just to brag

*and boast. How can a prophet learn it
in two decades slowly day by day?
Yet the one who learns it faster,
cannot stand up to pray? And we're
not mentioning the fard Salat, which
is hard for hypocrites. We're talking
about tahajjud the one that breeds
success. Each slave's test is different,
and fluctuates until their grown.
When harvest season comes to you,
then your tone will moan and groan.
You will clearly come to see what you
knew you had been shown. That your
knowledge and action was so little
thinking you'd be flown. But many
get thrown down for crimes they can't*

deny, because they hurt their soul inside and said everything was fine.

Yet what is undisputed is that Allah sent his book to you. You claim to have received it so what is your excuse? Did you not yet read it? Or do you lack Arabic? Because even non-Arabs obey commands when Allah makes the true faith stick.

Allah can change all creatures at any time decreed at any second. We do not know where we will be until announced for eternity. Though if you want to be happy then do what Allah expects. When you heard the message from your Lord did you treat

*it with respect? Allah sent you what
he wills and you will grow more over
time. Yet are you growing closer to or
farther from the fatherless Divine?
You criticize with fame those who
abuse Allah's names or attribute evil
sayings. But when have you once
lived a day in obedience free from sins
you crave? For the truly free is free
from sins all the rest are depraved and
enslaved. So what are you really a
slave to, today? Is it Allah's name?*

*How fast do you obey what you heard
and memorized? How faster do you
ally with your enemies in disguise?
Do you think your deeds are hidden,*

even if you fool yourself? Why then are you deluded about your sickly spiritual health? Had you not been so sick, my sanity would not be doubted.

This is what Allah made evident and I must repent. For we got confused from such advice to "balance things" and suffered ever since. May Allah bless all creatures, and increase their soul improvement. As we take a special exclusive test that many fools will fail. Many are in error, but they cannot be told how to tell. Hence Allah does not send bold warners equally globally to everyone, because the little they know already shows enough of what they won. Thus proving their case in advance of what more reminders would have done.

Don't destroy the blessings Allah sends you, or corrupt the Muslim hearts, by praising others than Allah for the wisdom Allah imparts. All repentance of all sinners is always lacking many parts. And when you realize your true danger, you will know where you should start. Allah will make you finish the rest of all your exam. But to pass this test with blessings will require extreme stress. You cannot relax a moment as you move closer to your death. So realize what's important to you yourself, constantly as you worship.

What's good for me may harm you. What's bad for you may help me. We do not know our destiny, but don't respond by making difficulty. Difficulty is defined as Allah has said repeatedly. You are not deaf or dumb or blind like others, so why do you act so sinfully? Or are you worse than all the rest and about to be punished painfully, both temporarily and Eternally.

This started as a correction intended to advise, and as Allah decrees all good deeds will always multiply.

*Truly worry with fear about yourself,
by acting according to Allah's letter.
This message is not the speech of
Allah, or even credited to a sinless
creature. It's not from an insane
person, as far as I can tell either. It
just rhymes a lot as destined to
improve the naseeha smell. The typer
may be worse than you, and can prove
it on qiyammah. As you know
already from their past pre-islamic
drama. Wasted life without Islam,
puts most far far ahead of me. But
Allah doesn't value quantity as much
as quality. And Arab Muslims have
potential for so much greater. So why
are we so different? Because many*

choose to play with fire and obey evil desires, despite already knowing better.

So if you like this letter then follow Allah's law. Don't ever sin on purpose and minimize your mistakes. Just sharing as a slave should do, don't complement my race. Start striving hard yourself as Allah desires haste. Perhaps you end up higher and I'll become a liar. Nobody is ever better because of inequality. If I can type such words today, tomorrow I can betray. Has it not happened to Iblis who said he was better than us all? Do you think Iblis has no case to make and just accepts his cursed fate? Perhaps Iblis may fail somewhat but many prove his claim. And those who do will get confused at faith levels they think insane.

So perhaps this will be fitna or ni'ma to cause some change. Yet since we talked about it, prioritizing time, I had to say we missed the mark, perhaps by divine design. It's not just our study minutes that fuel the upward climb. It's the deeds you do after what you know are sent to you as signs. I hope you get more blessings, without me losing mine.

Truly don't be thinking I'm as sincere, knowledgeable and special as the words may make me seem because majorly disrespectful irreligious sins are almost my habitual routine. We are not judged by what we show, but what Allah knows all about us. And sadly most prefer the ignorant judges because we fear just repercussions. Often we burn ourselves trying to save others from Hell to no avail at all, merely burning ourselves infecting our soul due to "good intentions" for others who fail. Never think any of these blessings are even partially deserved for I have more than fully earned Allah's powerful curse. Wise rhyming words like this just shows how faith is a fragile gift. As soon as you think you got it and are never letting go, it left your heart completely and you didn't even know. That's part of being human and part of being evil, which is only avoidable to those whom Allah blesses as was destined before the cradle. As when we're in our deep dark grave we will see how blind we were, when we see the crimes we did while divine signs were always there. Signs are never gone from life, we just ignore them because we're poor. Not poor in terms of money, but the poverty which the Prophets feared. For Muhammad *often supplicated not to disbelieve or be overcome with poverty that causes misery. Yet this great prophet died in debt and lived with starvation weakly. Though everyday he gave charity and at night prayed for his nation strongly. So what is true poverty according to prophetic definition? It is the poverty of spirituality that causes our damnation. The fiqh of the religion also known as understanding can come to non-Arabs if they obey Allah with true conviction sincerely. Those who memorize pages of Allah's book and write sins in their books of deeds, have truly not believed in those uncreated scriptures they frequently "love to read". They recite with such great melody while abusing what they say. Their hypocrisy is so deeply rooted they don't even know the meanings they deny. They may have fluent understanding yet keep falling into sin. While the one who learned to say one verse has practiced it better than the aforementioned accursed. And then when they read the next Juz the very next time they gain more ilm than the Huffaz. Truly I've read translations of the Quran more times than I can count, yet when I boosted true Taqwa by just a tiny amount, it was like I never read Quran before or ever heard such words or sounds.*

Every verse had deeper meaning that was locked before when I was cursed. Before I had hyper-focus and experienced such a thing, but that was totally different than actually reading and believing obediently. We read the book and sin disobeying what we read. Then we wonder asking Allah with cries why nobody listens to us or follows our lead? It is because our life is full of lies, on the outside and within. We lie so much throughout our limbs we don't count our sins as sins. Rather we think we're actually winning the battle with the devil when we grovel to his whims. We are like the people of past Scriptures who recited, invited and delighted, in prophetic teachings they had lost connection with. They said the words of guidance in both the Divine Speech sent to them and Prophetic wisdom. Yet the heart grew hard from hidden sins until everyone could see they were astray except them. And those who get to heaven don't live by such a playbook. They took the words of Allah to be truth and did what they were told to do. Such creatures were shaken to their core and remained shaking in slave-like obedience fearing the day they will be raised before their Lord. They won't be making false excuses or claiming to be self-guided good guys. Because the one who believes and then denies the blessing of their goodness is the devil's favorite prize. For once you count your blessings you failed to do your job, and then you may or may not feel it when faith leaves you. Then what will make you sob? When you lose it suddenly when will it ever return? For getting back to where you were is not guaranteed or ever earned. Any and every good deed is a blessed gift of increased faith from Allah that is impossible to return. While every sin you do is a loss of something more precious than life itself, whether you accept you fell or not, hell will come to those with poor spiritual health.

Don't think I am so special and blessed or am some friend of Allah guaranteed not to burn. Because even prophets taught to teach that faith in their prophetic goodness is mandatory to enter paradise, will fear the hellfire themselves because they are truly learned. It is those who have no fear for sins or corrupt intentions whose doom has been confirmed. Thus do what good you can while you can and maybe it might just continue and last through life long enough to get you what you want. But that is the whole problem is that you want anything at all. For a true slave worshipping Allah just hears and obeys the call. Whether that is the call of the Athan, to Tawheed, Taubah, Ikhlas, Jihad or on Qiyamah. It doesn't matter what it is, if it is a call from Allah then we must follow it all, for our survival.

You've done some nasty name-calling, to vent anger, having personal "fun" negatively insulting kafirs easing your own frustration. But the insults of what we may call fake gods or at least dumb snobs does damage. It doesn't damage devils, but hurts our ears and those of angels.

*Teach the ilm without bad flavor,
making the heart much purer, because
every day we exist to convey what
Allah says and not what we think or
favor. When we start to speak what
we feel, labeled as extra spice, our
tongues toxify the purest message
known making the valued truth not as
nice. Your intentions may be right,
but we all constantly lose blessed
sight of the God-given goal for doing
good deeds at all. The biggest success
to get as an author in this dunya life
is to not painfully edit the eternal
book of deeds we write. And do not
think it is only a visual book without
audio sounds or smells. For when*

you see all your deeds factually recorded you will be amazed at your poor grades. You were informed about the day when you'd get to see each and every deed, so why didn't you do each and every deed in a pure perfect way that would get you saved?

By getting infatuated with yourself ingratitude grows even as you strive to get better. Because by not following one uncreated letter of Allah's instructions, you just disobeyed the Creator. So what if you do so and you know it, while claiming to be a "Believer"? Such fools believe in mythology and a false Allah who *will teach them soon, what true Taqwa and Sincere Salafiyyah really is when it's the Day of Doom! And anger at others will not benefit yourself when Allah is angry at you and nothing saves you and you have no wealth to spend. By wealth I mean good deeds you saved for which to pay your debts that Day. So if you truly believe in Allah you must do so much more than pray. You say you run towards paradise but you know inside you're fake. You claim to not be spiritually asleep but you've never been awake! If not today then when? How much longer will you wait? For preparing now is your only chance for the day the earth will quake. Your grave will be opened soon and you will come out unprepared. But that's not shocking anyone, what's shocking is that you entered it unprepared.*

The sad part about advice is that when it's disobeyed it counts against you. The rhyme melodies that chime so nice will be dreaded if you go through life heedless. For when you die there is nothing else, not one more thing which you can do more. You nearly wasted all your life so far and are about to meet your Lord! What good did you do? What bad have you done? What more will you do for fun? On what day will you live your life as though you are going to die?